Like A Tree

Words to Stand On

Yelva S. Burley

1

ISBN: 978-0615869940

Printed in the United States of America

Published by:

Speak Life Publishing, LLC
P.O. Box 1144
Baltimore, MD 21203
www.yelvaburley.com

Front/Back Cover Images: Tyrone McBryde

Like A Tree
Words to Stand On

One of the joys of pastoring God's people is witnessing their development in the faith. Yes, it is one thing to see the pews full, but it is another thing to watch as people are becoming more and more "faith-full." Minister Yelva Burley happens to be one of those people. Indeed, her walk in the faith has been an authentic evolution. She has tackled real life issues; she has wrestled with the tensions related to faith, from which has been revealed to her the power of God, the goodness of God, and the reasons to remain faithful herself to God. *Like A Tree* is a microcosm of the fruit of her experience and we are blessed that she has taken the time to encourage us through this wonderful encouraging read.

Pastor Carl Solomon
United Baptist Church, Baltimore, MD

This book is destined to be a true blessing to all who are blessed to read it. The themes and devotions in this book are truly relevant to modern times. This book is not only enlightening, encouraging, educational, uplifting, spirit filled; I could go on and on but let me not forget to say exciting to read. It makes you take courage in knowing nothing you do for God will ever be in vain. This book encourages the reader to be faithful to his or her calling and to keep hope alive, regardless of their circumstances, so that they will receive the reward that comes from God in due time if they "faint not."

I earnestly believe that this book was written in harmony with God's will for Ms. Burley's life...While I'm waiting for her next book, I highly recommend this one to everyone. I'm proud to have this book on my shelf.

Pastor Bryan K. Merrick
Powerful Praises United Deliverance Church Baltimore, MD

Dedication

To my mother

Her prayers and encouragement help me
to stand.

Acknowledgements

Heavenly Father, thank You, for trusting me to suffer. All of it, I now know, was for Your glory and for my good.

A special thank you to a fantastic editing duo – Irishteen Thomas and Melissa Bradshaw. Your attention to detail blessed this project.

To my pastor, Dr. Carl J. Solomon, thank you. You are a disciple maker!

To the countless encouragers in my life, I am extremely grateful for the words you spoke over me, the prayers you lifted with me and for me, and the ways you showed yourself to be a disciple of Christ – oh what love!

Forward

When you've done all, just stand. Sometimes we get to a point where we've done all we can do, exhausted all of our resources and ideas, and there's nothing left to do - except Stand. Standing in the face of difficult circumstances is not easy. We are pulled, pushed, swayed, and knocked in all directions. We get physically weak, emotionally weak, and spiritually weak. We get frustrated one moment then expecting the next. We are high one moment then low the next. Or maybe it's just me. Maybe I'm the only Christian who's ever felt this way. Or maybe I'm not. I don't think I'm the only one who's felt this way. Let's just be honest from the start; in the midst of life's challenges, Christians must resolve within themselves that at some point in the storm, the only thing left to do is to just stand. We can't quit now. We can't throw in the towel. We can't raise the white flag. We can't end anything. We just have to stand. We stand until we see the salvation of the Lord. We stand until His will is clear. We stand until our prayers are manifested. We just STAND!

This book was written during a stormy season in my life and during the clean up process; I like to refer to it as the aftermath. It was written during months of consistent struggle, when one thing after another kept knocking at my door. My issues were cyclical, repetitious, malicious, and ferocious. There were some days when I struggled to believe that God was still with me, that He still loved me, and that He still had a plan for my life. Then I received a revelation. It came as I reflected on a storm I lived through in June of 2012. I didn't know it was coming but somehow, I had to go through it. As I journeyed home, I had a few passengers to drop off. The closer I got home to my sanctuary, my safe place, the worse conditions got. Trees were all over the place. The winds were blowing and the rains were blinding. It was a dangerous night to be out. The streets were dark, roads were flooded, and debris was everywhere. I did say it was a dangerous night, didn't I? Yet, I had to go through the mess to get home. I had to go through the storm.

As I traveled home, I was amazed by the trees that stood tall. Some trees didn't budge in the storm. They weren't uprooted. They endured and outlasted the storm. Some months later, in a prayer moment, the Father spoke to me about those trees. Through our time together, He revealed to me that trees with strong roots, that are well nourished, survive storms. I determined that I wanted to be like those trees. I wanted to be like a tree whose roots are so deep in God, so nourished by His word, that I stand, and when I've done all, I just stand (Ephesians 6:13). That was the key for me. My storm wasn't over at the time I began writing this book; however, I found new strength to keep moving forward in God. I rediscovered my Anchor, my Rock, My Sustainer, My God. He's been with me all along. He never left. And He's there with you too in whatever state you're in today. He's there with you in the storm, in your pain, in your disappointment, in your heartache, and in your frustration. He's even with you in your sin. He's in it all, in it until the end. Know that your storm won't last forever. It does have an expiration date. And as I stand through my storms, may you stand through yours, encouraged and empowered to keep on standing, **Like A Tree**. This phrase became my mantra. It's what I do now. It describes what I have to do during my storms. **Like A Tree** reveals my faith position. It reveals my faith posture. And it reveals God's promise. And praise God, all of His promises are Yes and in

Christ Jesus, we should all speak the amen (2 Corinthians 1:20)!

Contents

- Deliverance Is Mine
- Unshakeable
- Oh Temptation
- How Bad Do You Want It
- It's Not About You
- Encourage Yourself
- Good Ground
- He Will
- Don't Go Back
- Do It God's Way
- Get Ready to Die
- Hide Me
- Relentless
- Stop The Pity Party
- Bipolar
- Look Up
- Go to Jesus
- You Gave Me A New Song
- It's Coming

Introduction

There will be glory after this! Have you ever been so deep in a situation that you couldn't see how God could possibly get any good out of it? Well I'm not ashamed to admit that I had several days like that. There were some days that I didn't sense that God was near. And still there were some days that I wondered if He cared. *"Yet my soul refused to die."* When I couldn't see a way out and my mind and body was ever so weary, the Spirit whispered the words of Psalm 1:1-3 to me:

*Blessed is the one who does not walk in step with the wicked or stand in the way that sinners take or sit in the company of mockers, but whose delight is in the law of the LORD, and who meditates on his law day and night. That person is **like a tree** planted by streams of water, which yields its fruit in season and whose leaf does not wither— whatever they do prospers.*

This psalm is what God placed in my heart during a season of extreme testing and prolonged waiting. This song became one of the many scriptures that I "stood" on and it has become my banner and the premise of this book.

As I've "stood" on God's word and the strength of our relationship, I am ever more convinced about three things with regard to the struggles of life: they serve an eternal purpose, the children of God will survive them all, and in the midst of troubling times, God is always in control.

"You have enough word in you to deal with your situation." My pastor, Carl Solomon said these words one day. They revolutionized the way I was thinking. These few words reminded me that I had enough to make it through. The gift God gave me by grace, through His spirit, would not be quenched. My fire would not go out. My voice, the voice God gave me would not be silenced. God has blessed this book from beginning to end and declared unto me and to you, that whatever you're in, whatever you're going through, "There will be glory, after this." You can make it but in order to make it, you have to be able and willing to stand!

Standing requires patience. It requires enduring like a good soldier. Standing requires faith and works. Standing is denying yourself, taking up your cross, and following the Lord, no matter how you feel, no matter what happens.

My prayer is that through Like A Tree, you are spiritually blessed to keep on waiting, working, worshipping, and witnessing. Your storm will pass but in the meanwhile, you can stand, *Like A Tree*.

Let's journey together through these words to stand on. Use the *Personal Reflection* section after each devotion, allow the word to work on you. Allow the Holy Spirit to minister to your heart and mind. Don't move on too fast. Meditate on each word and I promise you, you won't face the next storm the same way you did your last. Now let's stand!

Hardships often prepare ordinary people
for an extraordinary destiny.
C.S. Lewis

Don't Wave That Flag

God began doing a good work in you, and I am sure he will
continue it until it is finished when Jesus Christ comes
again.
Philippians 1:6 NCV

When I talk to suffering Christians, I walk away from
the conversation either encouraged or discouraged. I'm
encouraged by Christians who know how to put the
word on their problems. I'm encouraged by people who
understand that weeping lasts for a night and that joy
comes in the morning. But I'm discouraged when people
who say they believe God with one breathe and then in
the next they exalt the devil. I'm discouraged by
Christians who are pessimistic and controlled by a spirit
of fear.

Suffering happens to the just and to the unjust. I've
discovered the purpose of our suffering. The enemy isn't
satisfied with just taking our stuff or messing with our
health or our family. His intent is to beat us down so
bad that we give up. He wants us to quit. He wants us
to quit believing in God's love and His influence in the
earth. He wants us to quit on our assignment, our
purpose. He wants us to wave the white flag and say I'm
done! That's it! That's His goal.

If God has gifted you to encourage, the enemy will
burden you with personal situations that are
discouraging. If you're gifted to teach and preach, the
enemy will burden you with situations that challenge
your faith in the One you teach and preach about. Look
at where you are frustrated the most. Does this
frustration impact other areas of your life? Have you

stopped doing something in the kingdom as a result of it? If so, this is where you have to press harder. You can't wave the white flag until all of the good work that God has begun in you has performed.

Personal Reflection

It's not the load that breaks you down; it's the way you carry it.

Lena Horne

Spiritual Pruning

"I am the true vine, and my Father is the gardener. He cuts off every branch in me that bears no fruit, while every branch that does bear fruit he prunes so that it will be even more fruitful. I am the vine; you are the branches. If you remain in me and I in you, you will bear much fruit; apart from me you can do nothing."

John 15:1-2, 5

I finally got to the point when I asked God why? I asked Him to show me the purpose for all of this pain and disappointment. I wanted to know what the benefit was or would be. I wanted to see the end. But God didn't show me how things were going to end up. Not yet. But what He did show me was the purpose. The purpose for my pain and your pain sometimes is for us. I love the figurative language Jesus uses in John 15. He tells us that God is the gardener, that He is the vine and that we are the branches. The branch is not without purpose; every branch produces something and if it doesn't, then it is worthless. Jesus explains to the disciples that in order for the branch to produce, it has to be pruned or cut to produce. The old is cut away to make room for the new. This is what happens to us. Our pruning process is uncomfortable. And let's just be real about it; it hurts! Pruning is inconvenient. Pruning sometimes lasts longer than we want. It may be humiliating. It will make us cry sometimes. Spiritual pruning will make us wonder is God really for us. Pruning will make us wonder why we still believe in God. But Jesus said that pruning produces. That means that the cut won't end in death. When we're pruned by the Father, it's not for our destruction; it's for increase. Jesus announced that the one who endured spiritual pruning would produce much fruit and the last time I checked the Book, Jesus never lied!

Personal Reflection

For I am convinced that neither death nor life, neither angels nor demons, neither the present nor the future, nor any powers, neither height nor depth, nor anything else in all creation, will be able to separate us from the love of God that is in Christ Jesus our Lord.

Romans 8:38-39

Never

"Never will I leave you; never will I forsake you."

Hebrews 13:5

The word "never" is so firm, so stern, so certain, so absolute. I remember when I was growing up, grown folks used to tell us that we should never say words like always and never. "Nothing is always or never," they would say. Yet the writer of Hebrews uses the word "never" twice in this one passage. As I meditated on this scripture I wondered if the intention of the double use of the word never was to make sure that God's children got a full revelation of God's great faithfulness and trustworthiness. Follow me for a moment. Desertion isn't a new phenomenon. Parents leave children every day. Husbands leave wives and wives leave husbands. Friends turn their backs on friends and family members fall-out with each other on a regular basis. That's nothing new. The reality is this - people leave people all the time. Yet God wants us to know a powerful truth and that is this – He is not like man. God does not act like nor does He react like human beings. He doesn't grow tired of us and He won't move on when we fail to satisfy Him. He won't leave us and He won't forsake us. So what does that really mean? It means that He won't leave us. Period. There is nothing that can separate us from His love (Romans 8:31). There's nothing that we could do that would make Him turn His back on us. Nothing! Think of the worst thing you've done. Play that scenario over and over again. No matter how rotten, disobedient, or stubborn you were, God didn't leave you. If you're in a pit, or a cave, or the lion's den He still won't leave you. When you're sick or frustrated or

22

unfaithful, He still won't leave you and He still won't forsake you. When you feel deserted, when you feel all alone, pull yourself up with and stand on these words, "Never will I leave you; never will I forsake you."

Personal Reflection

Focus on the purpose not the pain. God has a purpose for the trial you are in.

Dr. Tony Evans

Purposeful Pain

Now I want you to know, brothers and sisters, that what
has happened to me has actually served to advance the
gospel. As a result, it has become clear throughout the
whole palace guard and to everyone else that I am in
chains for Christ.

Philippians 1:12-13

Why do Christians suffer? I asked myself this question
one day when I was in the midst of a storm. I was
having a pity party, wondering why an all-loving God
would allow so much pain in my life. I knew I wasn't
perfect, that I had on occasion fallen short of His word
but I also knew that if I confessed my sins to God, that
He is faithful and just to forgive me and cleanse me
from all unrighteousness (1 John 1:9). I discovered that
sinfulness wasn't the result of my pain. I struggled. I
struggled even though I tried to be faithful over the few
things. I struggled even though I blessed the Lord at all
times and His praise was continually in my mouth. I
struggled even though I did sought, first His kingdom
and His righteousness. I struggled even though I trusted
God, with everything that was in me; I trusted Him! Yet,
I struggled. Then one day I stumbled upon this
scripture. It was familiar to me but this time, it had new
meaning. This scripture gave me what I needed in the
storm.

The apostle Paul knew a lot about suffering. He knew
about persecution. He knew about spiritual and
natural storms. He knew about being in prison; he
knew about being in chains. Paul understood
something over two thousand years ago that I needed to

know if I was going to stand through my storms. Paul knew that there was purpose in his pain. Paul knew that the pain in his life was not intended to kill him nor stop him. Paul knew that the pain in his life and in ours is allowed so that in some way, at an appointed time, our pain, our story, would serve to advance the gospel. We survive the tough seasons in our lives so that we can tell others how we made it through. The beginning, middle, and end of our story should always point to Christ. Our story should cause others to see Him better. Our pain has purpose. So the next time you hurt, know that your pain is in God's will – for at some point, your situation will become the pathway to someone else's deliverance.

Personal Reflection

Change your thoughts and you change your life.

Yelva Burley

Get Yourself Together

If you fall to pieces in a crisis, there wasn't much to you in the first place.

Proverbs 24:10 (Msg)

... if you're worn out in this footrace with men, what makes you think you can race against horses? And if you can't keep your wits during times of calm, what's going to happen when troubles break loose like the Jordan in flood?

Jeremiah 12:5 (Msg)

Sometimes you're going to have to confront yourself. There will be a time, if not multiple times when we have to stop and "check ourselves before we wreck ourselves." This is an old saying that describes Christian responsibility. We are responsible for ourselves. When trouble comes our way it's tempting to cave in under the pressure, especially when one bad thing after another happens to us. It's not unusual for Christians to give up, to quit fighting the good fight of faith. It's not unusual for Christians to be depressed, to have nervous breakdowns, and to fall apart. Solomon wrote, "If you fall to pieces in a crisis, there wasn't much to you in the first place." And Jeremiah wrote, "... if you're worn out in this footrace with men, what makes you think you can race against horses? And if you can't keep your wits during times of calm, what's going to happen when troubles break loose like the Jordan in flood?" Ouch! These verses are our wake up calls. These verses force us to evaluate our faith posture when we're going through. Are we taking the punches with the best of them or are we down for the count? These verses should convict us and they should compel us – compel us to get ourselves together. We must shake ourselves loose of whatever weight is holding us down. Whatever the weight might be, hopelessness or helplessness or something else – shake it lose. We're in a race and only those who endure until the end are going to win.

Personal Reflection

If you want God to bless you and use you greatly, you must be willing to walk with a limp the rest of your life, because God uses weak people.

Rick Warren

Please Remove These Thorns

...Therefore, in order to keep me from becoming conceited, I was given a thorn in my flesh, a messenger of Satan, to torment me. Three times I pleaded with the Lord to take it away from me. But he said to me, "My grace is sufficient for you, for my power is made perfect in weakness." Therefore I will boast all the more gladly about my weaknesses, so that Christ's power may rest on me. That is why, for Christ's sake, I delight in weaknesses, in insults, in hardships, in persecutions, in difficulties. For when I am weak, then I am strong.

2 Corinthians 12:7b-10

When we're going through, I mean when we're really going through we pray like Paul prayed, "Lord, take it away!" When we've had about all we think we can take, we cry out like Paul in pain and frustration, "please remove these thorns." This reminds me of roses. Roses are so beautiful and smell so fragrant. But roses are connected to vines that are prickly. Rose bushes have thorns. The thorns don't take away from the rose's beauty or purpose. However, the thorns must be handled delicately. They must be handled with care. God created roses and He created the rose bush, thorns and all. Paul wanted his thorns removed and God told him no! His thorn and our thorn serve a purpose in our spiritual maturity. Thorns don't have to stop us. Like the rose, thorns make us who we are. In fact, they manifest the power of God in our lives. Thorns remind us that we are not all sufficient; God is. Thorns remind us that we are not all-powerful; God is. Thorns remind us of our neediness of God, our helplessness. He is the one who enables us to accomplish great feats. He is the one, through Jesus Christ, who gives us the victory, the ability to make wealth, and to have life more abundantly. As you're going through, remember that God's grace is more than enough. His power is made perfect when you're weak, not when you're strong. You can live with the thorns in your life. You can prosper in spite of them. You can experience the peace of God with thorns. You are more than a conqueror with your thorns. You are fearfully and wonderfully made, with your thorns. You are loved, accepted, and gifted, with your thorns. You are complete, with your thorns. So the next time you are tempted to ask God to remove them, remember Paul. Remember that your thorns don't make you weak; they make you strong.

Personal Reflection

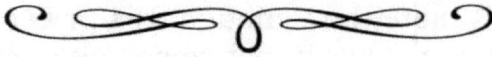

The Lord will work out his plans for my
life...

Psalm 138:8 (NLT)

Trouble Won't Last Always

For our light and momentary troubles are achieving for
us an eternal glory that far outweighs them all.

2 Corinthians 4:17

The apostle Paul knew how to paint a picture. He wrote
with such imagery and relevancy. Sometimes his words
make us shout for joy and sometimes, his words pierce
our hearts – convicting us. As a suffering servant, he
was always mindful that being a disciple of Christ has
its costs. He knew about being persecuted for Christ's
sake. He knew about being lied on and imprisoned. He
knew about being beaten because he declared Jesus is
Lord. Paul knew about pain. He knew about the cost of
discipleship. So he's a great spokesperson about pain
and in this particular scripture, Paul lets us know
several things about our struggles. One, our struggles
are light. Now he's not saying what we're going through
doesn't hurt or that it's not difficult but he is saying
that the pain we endure today is nothing compared to
what we're going to get out of it. There are eternal
ramifications connected to our troubles. They are not
working against us. On the contrary, the storms of this
life are working for us. Secondly, he lets us know that
our struggles are for a moment, they last for a season.
Whatever you're going through is temporary. Our
troubles have an expiration date. There is a God
prepared date for us to come out of our dark places. Our
trouble won't last always. The trouble your family is
going through will end one day. Your financial struggles
will end one day. The pain in your body, it's going to be
gone one day. "Our light and momentary troubles are
achieving for us an eternal glory that far outweighs

them all!" Hold on my brother; hold on my sister, a change is going to come.

Personal Reflection

Without faith it's impossible to speak life.
Yelva Burley

Move this Mountain

He replied, "Because you have so little faith. Truly I tell you, if you have faith as small as a mustard seed, you can say to this mountain, 'Move from here to there,' and it will move. Nothing will be impossible for you."

Matthew 17:20

Have you ever faced a situation, which, on the surface, seemed too hard for God? Now I know that you may be a born again Christian, Holy Ghost filled, and fire baptized, but have you ever once thought that your situation was too big for your God? I know that you may have been raised in the church, served on the choir or on the deaconess board, or even taught Sunday School but have you ever looked at your situation and thought, there's no way this can change; it's too late? Maybe I'm the only one. But I don't think so. The mountains in our way can appear to be so enormous, so insurmountable, so daunting, so overwhelming, and so beyond the point of changing. But they aren't. The mountains in our lives are only as big as we make them. Please don't think that I'm minimizing the seriousness of your situation. Your sickness is real. Your financial issues are real. Your relationship struggles are real. I have experienced some real crisis in my life too; I understand your stress, I understand your worry. I understand your anger. I understand. But, and there's always a "but", your mountains and my mountains can be moved.

Whether the meaning of this scripture should be interpreted literally or figuratively, I believe Jesus wants the body of Christ to see a truth in this passage. The truth is simple: when we believe, miracles will happen. A mountain moving would require God to perform a miracle. Some of our situations require God to do something, something supernatural. Some of our concerns are beyond the assistance of our friends and loved ones. Some of our issues are beyond specialists. Many of our deepest concerns require the divine intervention of almighty God! We just have to believe. Our faith activates the uncommon. Our faith is the catalyst for change. Our faith moves mountains. Like the small mustard seed, your faith has the potential to produce beyond its small beginnings.

Personal Reflection

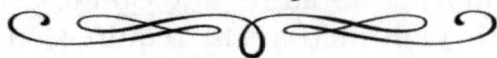

Only GOD can take a set-back and make
it work out for your GOOD.

Yelva Burley

For My Good

It was good for me to be afflicted so that I might learn your decrees.

Psalm 119:71

As a child, I remember hearing these fated words, "This is going to hurt me more than you." And I remember thinking, yeah right! Parents correct their children because they love them. Correction isn't easy on the person giving the correction. Oftentimes we only look at the pain of the correction from our point of view. However, I believe that God does not celebrate whenever He has to correct His children. Yet, correction is for our good. God is forever-loving. He chastises those that He loves. God doesn't rejoice when bad things happen to us. However, because He's God, He's not wasteful either. He takes the pain and strains in our lives and uses them for our good. That rejection you suffered, at the hands of people so close, so intimate with you, it was for your good.

No one likes or welcomes suffering. No one raises their hand and volunteers to go through. No one points to themselves and says, "I've got next." No one. And although Jesus obeyed His father, I don't believe He was gung ho about going to the cross.

LaShaun Pace sings a song that reminds me of the benefit of going through. She says that all the hurt and pain, all that she endured was for her good and for God's glory. The songstress helps us to put our pain in perspective. It is good for us to go through. Many of us learned who God is as a result of going through. Some

46

of us learned how to pray God's word as a result of going through. So, we can declare like the songstress, it was all for my good!

Personal Reflection

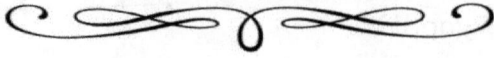

Your season of struggle may be your
season of testing.
                                    Yelva S. Burley

Accept What God Allows

… Shall we accept good from God, and not trouble?" In all this, Job did not sin in what he said.

Job 2:10

There are so many lessons that derive from the life of Job. His struggle speaks! Today as I recuperate physically, mentally and spiritually this scripture ministered to my weary soul. I had actually read this scripture earlier in the day but it wasn't until I had seen it a few hours later that I tuned my ears to what the Spirit had to say. Yesterday I heard clearly, "Accept what God allows." I wasn't thinking about Job but I was thinking about my own miserable circumstance. In my devotions I was led to the story of Job. I needed to know how he handled loss, repetitive, seemingly cyclical loss. I read his story and felt his pain. I connected with his loss. I knew personally how it felt to keep getting bad news. Job's story encouraged me to keep getting up and to keep on living.

Job said something that remains with me today. He said, "Shall we accept good from God and not trouble?" We praise God when our pockets are full and the world is right with us but what do we do when the rains keep pouring in our lives? What do we do when we don't seem to be getting any breaks? How do we handle life when life seems to be mishandling us? I looked at Job's response as my wakeup call! I internalized his response and allowed it to be my motivation to keep on moving. I had to accept what God allows. This trouble does not change who God is; He's still God; He's still holy and worthy of praise. And I can't allow my trouble to change who I am in Him.

What do you do when you don't know why?

Personal Reflection

Speaking life over yourself and others requires the mind of Christ, the word of God, and the ability to see beyond your current reality.

Yelva Burley

Yes You Can

Whatever I have, wherever I am, I can make it through
anything in the One who makes me who I am.
Philippians 4:13 (Msg)

For many, this is a familiar scripture. I've encouraged
myself as well as others with it on occasion. I taught it
to my children when they were very young. I've heard it
preached, seen it on t-shirts, bookmarks, journals, bags
and more. I have it displayed on several things in my
home. It's a mighty word to stand on. "I can" is a
powerful statement. In a world where we're told we
can't or we even think we can't, these words, "I can"
supply strength to the weary soul. I love this
translation of the scripture because of these two words-
whatever and wherever. In Christ, you and I can make it
through whatever life brings. In Christ, you and I can
make it through wherever life takes us. Whatever means
bankruptcy, poverty, cancer, divorce, and depression.
Whatever! Wherever means unemployment lines,
hospitals, doctors' offices, and dead-end jobs. Name the
situation, name the place and the word says, whatever
and wherever – you can make it through. Think of any
crisis and this word says, "you can make it through."
Trouble may be knocking at your door right now. Your
trial doesn't matter. You can make it through. The
power of this word over your "whatever and wherever"
remains the same. Find peace in this word. Find
comfort in this word. Find joy in this word. Find faith
in this word. Find strength in this word. Stand on this
word. Build or rebuild your life on it. Jesus, the One
who makes us who we are, empowers us to make it

54

through- alive, well, and victorious. Let me speak this over you, "Yes you can!"

Personal Reflection

Other people are going to find healing in your wounds. Your greatest life messages and your most effective ministry will come out of your deepest hurts.

Rick Warren

For His Glory

"You are the light of the world. A town built on a hill cannot be hidden. Neither do people light a lamp and put it under a bowl. Instead they put it on its stand, and it gives light to everyone in the house. In the same way, let your light shine before others, that they may see your good deeds and glorify your Father in heaven.

Matthew 5:14-16

I read a devotion today that reminded me of one of my roles in the kingdom of God. This devotion reminded me of my calling, the very purpose God called me to preach the gospel of Jesus Christ. That purpose was, is, and will always be to show forth God's glory. God called me to reveal Him, through His Son, to the earth. To do this, God empowered me with gifts, His unmerited favor, and a heart for Him and people. God's goodness and His gifts make me appealing. They draw people to me. However, this scripture keeps me grounded. It reminds me of my kingdom place. Even when I'm going through I stand on this scripture and ask myself, is God being revealed through me in this situation. Name any great person of the Bible and I can guarantee you he or she experienced blessing and struggle. Yet through it all, they showed forth God's glory. When blessed, they showed forth God's glory. When struggling, they showed forth God's glory. They understood that the kingdom wasn't about them.

Can you stand to be an Aaron or a Jonathan? Can you stand to be a Naomi or an Elizabeth? Can you stand to be like John the Baptist, understanding that your role, your influence is only to put someone else in the spotlight? Can you handle it if your name isn't called or your service isn't acknowledged? Can you handle being a servant who lets his or her light shine through everyday living so that God can be seen and glorified? Can you?

Personal Reflection

If you live with chickens but think like an eagle, it's only a matter of time before someone will see the eagle in you and allow you to spread your wings and fly higher. Be patient.

Bishop T.D. Jakes

I Shall Rise

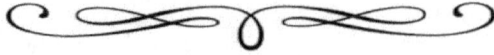

He gives strength to the weary and increases the power
of the weak. Even youths grow tired and weary, and
young men stumble and fall; but those
who hope in the LORD will renew their strength. They
will soar on wings like eagles; they will run and not grow
weary, they will walk and not be faint.

Isaiah 40:29-31

This is one of my favorite scriptures. Whenever I hear it
or read it I'm instantly comforted; I know that I'm going
to make it. Every time I hear or read this scripture my
mind is renewed and I feel, deep down in my soul that I
can go on. The Spirit of the Lord whispers this word to
me when my load gets too much to bear. I know that
Jesus said that we can cast all our cares upon Him and
we'll find rest but I believe that sometimes, the load will
stay on us so that we can find our strength and power
in God alone. I believe that God wants His children to be
constantly reminded that He is our strength giver and
our power source. Why else would the word of God tell
us that He gives strength to the weary and increase the
power of the weak? Why else would the word of God tell
us that He renews the strength of those who put their
hope in Him? Why else would the word of God tell us
that He makes provision for us to soar, to not grow
weary, and to not faint?

We're living in a time in which energy drinks and all
kinds of home remedies are used to give jolts of instant
energy. There's a pill for this and a pill for that. There's
a powder for this and a powder for that. These methods
for increasing stamina are temporary fixes. They wear
off eventually and we find ourselves needing another five

hour boost. Yet the word of God reminds us that the Lord our God provides our strength and increases our power. When we stand in the strength and power of God, we are rejuvenated, refreshed, and ready to keep going, to keep standing. Standing in and through the storms of life can leave us weather-beaten and weak but God promises through this word that you and I can soar; we can soar like the eagle; we can rise.

Personal Reflection

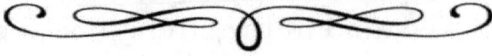

You can't get much done in life if you only work on the days when you feel good.

Jerry West

Work While You Wait

The warden paid no attention to anything under Joseph's care, because the LORD was with Joseph and gave him success in whatever he did.

Genesis 39:23

Joseph is an excellent example of a waiting servant. This dreamer, slave, and God-follower had two visions. In both visions (dreams), people were bowing down to him. They were subject to him. He saw himself elevated. He saw himself ruling over even his family members. The announcement of these dreams to his family resulted in him being sold into slavery, being falsely accused, and being imprisoned. But God gave him a dream. Don't you just love the way God leaves out the details? I used to wonder about that. I used to wonder why God didn't show Joseph the whole picture, the ends and the out. Joseph didn't see the whole process or the journey he'd have to travel before the vision would become a reality. As I've grown in faith, I've discovered that the details aren't as important as the promise. Joseph believed God and he acted on his faith. He lived like he believed in what God said. Our problem sometimes is in the waiting. God shows us something or tells us something and we think that it's supposed to happen immediately or overnight. Joseph's process took over ten years. Yet, he didn't grow weary in his well doing. He knew he was going to reap a harvest if he didn't give up. So he did what every believer should do while they are waiting on God; he worked. He worked while he waited. And he worked well, I might add. He didn't complain while he waited. He didn't get frustrated while he waited. Waiting on the Lord doesn't give us a license to become complacent. Waiting on God to show up and show off doesn't give us permission to sit and twiddle our thumbs. We've got to work! While you're waiting on God to move on your behalf, work. Work well. You'll discover, as Joseph did, that God will bless you along the way.

Personal Reflection

My hope is built on nothing less
Than Jesus' blood and righteousness;
I dare not trust the sweetest frame,
But wholly lean on Jesus' name.
On Christ, the solid Rock, I stand;
All other ground is sinking sand.

Lyrics from My Hope Is Built On Nothing
Less
Edward Mote

Stand On It

God is not human, that he should lie, not a human being, that he should change his mind. Does he speak and then not act? Does he promise and not fulfill?

Numbers 23:19

During a very difficult time in my life I stood very firmly on this word. I stood so hard on it I decided that I would go through one of my Bibles (the new pretty one) and highlight every scripture that I planned to pray often and believe God would manifest for me. Then I decided that I would put tabs on the pages for easy access. It was my banner of faith. People examined my Bible, thinking the tabs were there to signify the books of the Bible. They were surprised to discover that the tabs represented scriptures of faith, the very words of God that I believed, the very words of God that kept me alive. These scriptures became my Promise Book and many are now the driving force of this book. I confidently spoke these scriptures into the atmosphere in the morning, noon, and night. I prayed them, memorized them, studied them, but most of all, I believed each and every one of them. If you are going to be able to stand, you have to trust that God can and will do what He says. He's not like a man or a woman; he's all together trustworthy. He keeps his word. God won't change up on you. He's not a promise breaker. He won't change His mind about the word or words He gave you. His word is His word and each one is reliable, active and alive. There isn't a single word in the Bible that will not accomplish what He intended for it to accomplish (Isaiah 55:11). Each word will come to pass; each word will be fulfilled. The word of God is truth - it won't be or can't be altered, nothing added, nothing taken away. You can and should stand on it with confidence and assurance! Stand on the word of God that declares you are more than a conqueror (Romans 8:37). Stand on the word that declares that you will know the truth and the truth will make you free. Stand on the word that says that our God shall supply all your needs according to His riches in glory in Christ Jesus (Phil 4:19). Stand on His word that declares that God, in all His power and infinite wisdom, knows how to work every circumstance together for your good (Romans 8:28). These are just a few "words" to stand on. Find yours and cling to them, until you see with your eyes what you've read and declared.

Personal Reflection

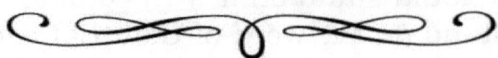

Persistence –
steadfastness, endurance, tenacity, grit,
stamina, resolution, indefatigability,
constancy, backbone, drive, immovability,
determination
Does this describe you?

Persist

Consider it pure joy, my brothers and sisters, whenever you face trials of many kinds, because you know that the testing of your faith produces perseverance. Let perseverance finish its work so that you may be mature and complete, not lacking anything.

James 1:2-4

Followers of Christ, who persist under trials and tests of many kinds, develop spiritual muscle. I'm not a fitness guru but I do know what happens when someone begins strength training. It's painful! There's often soreness and weakness involved. But if one keeps at it, muscles begin to develop. What once caused pain eventually fades away. With continued training, people become stronger.

This scripture in James shows us that something similar occurs in the spirit as we face tests. Eventually the testing of our faith produces persistence and when we've persisted long enough, we become mature-not lacking anything. So persist! The benefits are well worth the struggle.

The issue that many of us have with persisting is that persistence requires time, discipline, and submission. Persistence requires time. If what we needed from God came instantaneously, there would be no need to persist or to endure in the faith. Persistence requires discipline. In order to persist in the faith, we must develop and maintain spiritual discipline. What do I mean by this? Well, we have to consistently pray. We have to faithfully serve. We have to live obediently to the word of God. We have to fast. Yes, we have to turn our plates down. We have to study to show ourselves approved. We have to suffer like good soldiers, not like people who are tossed by every issue that comes our way. We like to think we know what's best. We like to think that we have all the answers. If only this would happen. But the truth is, we don't know what's best for us. God's wisdom is infinite. He has you right where he needs you, right where He wants you. The good news is that at the end of this process, you'll be mature and complete, not lacking anything. Endure the wait. Submit to God's timing. And above all, commit yourself to persist!

Personal Reflection

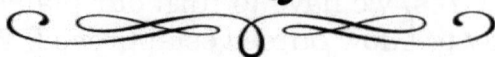

When my life is spinning, when things and people get demanding, I stop and remember my Center.

Yelva Burley

More Than Anything

Then he fell to the ground in worship and said: "Naked I came from my mother's womb, and naked I will depart. The LORD gave and the LORD has taken away; may the name of the LORD be praised."

Job 1:20-21

Job is one of several champions of suffering. The beginning of the book that bears his name chronicles his background, how he reverenced God and turned away from evil. We discover that Job is wealthy, a successful entrepreneur. He and his wife have several children; Job is living the life. Yet despite his love and obedience, Job lost everything. In the span of one day he went from "blinging" to bankruptcy. Before he had a chance to process and mourn one loss, a messenger came to tell him about another loss.

Isn't that just like life, one thing after another. I've been there and I know, in a way, what Job must have felt like. I've had stormy seasons, seasons when it was one issue after another- one fire after another that needed to be extinguished. In the course of one year, I owned four cars. That's right, four cars! There was the car that was consumed in a vehicle fire. Then there was the car with only 4,000 miles on it that succumbed to flash flood waters. Then there was the car that was crashed into by a vehicle that failed to stop at a stop sign, one issue after another. In the midst of this there was underemployment, unemployment, health issues, and a lot of tears. Yet through my storms and yours we can't forget our God. Our situations change but He never does. He's the same, yesterday, today, and forevermore. Therefore our worship and adoration should remain the same. When you're well, worship Him. When you're sick, worship Him. When you're in a relationship, worship Him. When he or she walks out on you, worship God. Children of God must get to a place where they can love God more than anything. I think that's what Job shows us. He had a lot of stuff but when it was all taken from him, he realized that with God, he was still rich. Job cherished God more than his possessions, more than his family, more than his reputation. God was his treasure. Is He yours?

Personal Reflection

Weapons will be formed against you but take heart; they WILL NOT prosper!

Yelva Burley

I'm A Soldier

Put on the full armor of God, so that you can take your stand against the devil's schemes.

Ephesians 6:11

Sometimes we're going to be in the fight of our lives. The Lord never promised that our lives would be void of strains and pains. The word never said that we wouldn't have struggles. But it does say that we'll overcome them all. One of the ways we overcome our struggles is by taking on the characteristics of a soldier. Sometimes the forces of darkness pick fights with us. Sometimes those forces pick and pick and pick. As witnesses of Christ we are targets for the evil one. In prayer, I cried out to God and asked Him to help me fight my battles like a good soldier. This is what the Spirit revealed: the Christian must prepare for spiritual battles like a soldier prepares for war.

Fully prepared soldiers are mindful to dress like they are going to war. Paul gives a whole list of the dress code for spiritual battle: helmet of salvation, breastplate of righteousness, shield of faith, belt of truth, feet fitted with the preparation of the gospel, and the sword - which is the word of God. Going into battle without your battle clothes on will prove to be fatal.

Fully prepared soldiers talk like they're ready for war. As Christian soldiers we should be talking spiritual warfare when we're going through. Our struggles are not against flesh and blood. Fully prepared soldiers act like they're in a war, like they are in the fight of their lives. Soldiers don't give up; they don't give in until the mission is accomplished. Christian soldiers should do the same. There shouldn't be any quit in you, not until you have secured the victory, not until you see the salvation of the Lord. Fully prepared soldiers have a particular mindset. Their mindset is not on personal matters. They aren't focused on what they are going to eat or wear. They have one thing in mind, winning the war. When you're in the Army of the Lord, you have to have your mind on heavenly things. You have to ensure that you have the mind of Christ. That your mind is on the true, the noble, the right, the pure, the lovely... (Philippians 4:8). Oftentimes, our battles are not outside of us; they're in our minds. Are you ready to make war?

Personal Reflection

84

Faith is taking the first step even when
you don't see the whole staircase.
                    Dr. Martin Luther King, Jr.

With Blinders On

For we walk by faith, not by sight.
2 Corinthians 5:7(NKJV)

I'm a fan of crime television. I like programs that focus on finding out who did it. In these programs, the detectives follow the evidence. For them, the strength of their case lies in what they can see. Their quest to discover the evidence is very entertaining for me. I realize that these shows are only dramatizations of what actually occurs in our legal system. However, these programs reveal something that is very true for many people. They need to see it to believe it. Many people live their lives by sight and not by faith. "Show me and then I'll believe," is what they say. Build the building and then I'll come. I remember hearing statements like these many years ago and believing them to be true. "Seeing is believing." As a growing disciple, I now know that this phrase is totally contrary to the word of God. This way of thinking and living does not give power to the believer and it certainly doesn't prove faith in God. People who walk around waiting to see it before they believe it are walking around with blinders on. They are oblivious to the power that faith produces. They are hindered by the notion that faith comes by seeing. People who walk by sight are waiting for the next big thing to happen so they can jump on the bandwagon. Walking by sight does not please God. Faith pleases God (Hebrews 11:6). We can't declare a thing and see it established until we walk by faith. We can speak life over ourselves and others until we walk by faith and not by sight. So, walk by faith for your healing. Walk by faith for your family and your finances. Sight says that your marriage is breaking up but faith says that what God has joined together, let no one separate (Mark 10:9). Reality says that you have more bills than income but faith says that God knows you have need and will take care of you (Matthew 6:30). God has you. Take the blinders off and watch what He'll do.

Personal Reflection

Even if you fall on your face, you're still moving forward.

Victor Kiam

I Won't Let Go

Therefore, my dear brothers and sisters, stand firm. Let
nothing move you...
1 Corinthians 15:58

At some point in the struggle, the fire of affliction will
seem too turned up. The pressure will seem to be
unbearable. You'll begin to think you're burning up; this
is it. When you get to this point you have two choices:
you can either give up or you can press on. Disciple of
Christ, you must choose the latter. You can't give up.
Your purpose is tied to your pain. The temptation to
quit will be ever present, staring you in the face. The
temptation to quit will dare you to get up and keep
trying after you've faced rejection or what appears to be
failure. Quitting, at some point in the storm, appears to
be the only option left. So you contemplate throwing in
the towel more than you imagine yourself delivered.
Beloved, you must stand firm. Don't move! Endure this,
whatever your "this" is. Press on. Keep persevering.
Pursue the promises of God. Push, keep praying until
something happens. Praise God in the midst of it all.
And ponder. Consistently ponder or think on the
promises of God. Allow His promises to sure up the
ground that you are standing on. Allow them to be your
firm foundation, your only leg to stand on.   Your
relationship with the Lord and His word will become
your anchor, holding you down so that you don't sink
when the storms of life come crashing in on you. He
will hold you. He will keep your mind in perfect peace.
He will be your light and your salvation. He will be the
source of your strength when you get weak. Stay in

Him and you'll be able to stand, to let nothing move you. I guarantee you, the pain of your process will be worth it. It's through Jesus that you victory is secured. Your labor won't be in vain!

Personal Reflection

"For my thoughts are not your thoughts,
neither are your ways my ways,"
declares the LORD.

ISAIAH 55:8

An Unconventional God

So Naaman went with his horses and chariots and
stopped at the door of Elisha's house. Elisha sent a
messenger to say to him, "Go, wash yourself seven times
in the Jordan, and your flesh will be restored and you
will be cleansed." So he went down and dipped himself
in the Jordan seven times, as the man of God had told
him, and his flesh was restored and became clean like
that of a young boy.

2 Kings 5:9-10, 14

Oftentimes we look for God to do things the way we
imagine things ought to be done. It's easy for us who
claim to be spiritual to think that we are so righteous
that God considers our thoughts when He wants to
display His glory. The story of Naaman reminds me of
this. He was the head man in charge. The Bible says
that he was commander of an army, a great man in the
sight of his master, and a valiant soldier. However, this
great man had to deal with a great issue. He had a
painful skin disease called leprosy. One day Naaman
heard of a prophet that could heal him. He pressed his
way to find this man and when he got to the prophet
Elisha, he's told to go and wash in the Jordan, not by
the prophet but by a messenger. Naaman took offense
that the man of God didn't have the decency to see him
personally and call on the Lord on his behalf. And to
top it off, why did he have to wash in the dirty Jordan?
He left furious and it required some wise servants to
help him come to his senses. As I meditated on
Naaman's story, I began to see that some people want
"it" more than others. Some want the blessing without

the work. I questioned myself. I thought about how bad I wanted to be delivered. I confronted myself with the question, "What are you willing to do to get delivered?" Was I willing to do whatever God told me to do to be free? Was I willing to lay aside my title and influence and do something strange, to see the glory of God? What about you? Are you prepared to do whatever God tells you to do even if it requires you to step outside your comfort zone? Are you willing to accept that God might require you to participate in your own deliverance? Are you yielded enough to God's plan and purpose, for your life, to trust in His unconventional ways? The miracle you need may not come in the way that your finite mind imagines. The miracle you need may just come in an unconventional, never thought off, unfathomable way. Can you handle that?

Personal Reflection

"Then you will know the truth, and the truth will set you free."

John 8:32

Deliverance Is Mine

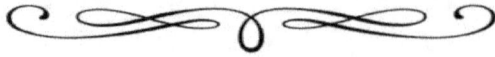

...He has sent me to bind up the brokenhearted, to proclaim freedom for the captives and release from darkness for the prisoners, to proclaim the year of the LORD's favor and the day of vengeance of our God, to comfort all who mourn, and provide for those who grieve in Zion— to bestow on them a crown of beauty instead of ashes, the oil of joy instead of mourning, and a garment of praise instead of a spirit of despair. They will be called oaks of righteousness, a planting of the LORD for the display of his splendor.

Isaiah 61:1-3

I was functioning but I did so without the normal excitement and joy. Everything I did I did without a sense of urgency. I knew something was wrong. I knew it was spiritual but I couldn't put my finger on it. I didn't think I was depressed. The trouble was I just "wasn't." I wasn't content; I wasn't sleeping; I wasn't focused. But then I "was." I was irritable, forgetful, and moody. I was up one moment and down the next. I wasn't having crazy thoughts but I was tired, very, very tired of my struggles. I couldn't figure it out. This wasn't the first time I'd struggled. It wasn't the first time bad things happened to me. I overcame them all! But it was the first time I couldn't move forward. Things got so bad that I became very indecisive. Simple tasks became so complicated. And talk about being a procrastinator. I was a major one! I was in need of deliverance. I just didn't know from what. During this time, a friend was sending motivational messages daily. She sent a message one day that made me smile. It was Isaiah 61:3. The oaks of righteousness caught my attention. A few days later I came across the index card that I wrote the scripture on and became curious about the text around this scripture. What was going on? It was in this scripture that my spiritual problem was revealed. All of my "symptoms" could be summed up in two words, spiritual heaviness. Everything was heavy for me. The spirit of heaviness manifested itself in complaining, hopelessness, weariness, and more. I was ashamed of where I let myself go. I felt guilty that I had gone so low. What I discovered was that this spirit is such a manipulator. It manipulated me into magnifying my problems and not God. My issues became center stage for me, with the horrific scenes playing over and over again. But I thank God for His word, for the revelation in His word - spiritual fights can only be won with spiritual weapons (2 Corinthians 10:4-5).

Personal Reflection

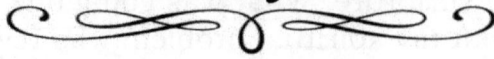

Faith activates God. Fear activates the enemy.

Joel Osteen

Unshakeable

Is anything too hard for the LORD?

Genesis 18:14

What do you do when you face a seemingly insurmountable problem? How do you respond to situations that appear to be unchangeable? What do you say when God declares a thing to you and it's totally contrary to your reality? These questions are important for the believer because we will all be forced to answer them one day. Just keep living! Your answer will depend on one thing only, do you believe in what God said? Is His word true to you? If you answered yes, then you can stand on this word. The question the angel asked Sarah is rhetorical. The angel already knew the answer. The question was meant to reveal Sarah's faith position. It was meant to challenge her, to get her to think outside the box. It was meant to take her faith in God to a new level, to help her look beyond the limitations of her existence and see a God who is not bound by the laws of physics nor logic.

Oftentimes, we are placed in situations where our faith must be challenged, where we have to be stretched. It's a test. The solution is simple. Trust God. Trust God in spite of your situation and because of your situation. Announce to your dilemma that you know that there is nothing too hard for God. Diseases are not too hard for God. Your lack is not too hard for God. Loneliness and depression is not too hard for God. Your disobedient child is not too hard for God. The atheist, the alcoholic, the prostitute, the gang banger, the lazy, the unforgiving, the worst of the worst is not too hard for

God. Imagine your hard thing right now. No matter how unchangeable or irreversible it may seem, declare that it is not too hard for your God. Now wait in faith. Expect God to do something. Let nothing move you; let nothing shake you.

Personal Reflection

What a wretched man I am! Who will rescue me from this body that is subject to death? Thanks be to God, who delivers me through Jesus Christ our Lord!

Romans 7:24-25

Oh Temptation

The only temptation that has come to you is that which everyone has. But you can trust God, who will not permit you to be tempted more than you can stand. But when you are tempted, he will also give you a way to escape so that you will be able to stand it.

(1 Corinthians 10:13 NCV)

No test or temptation that comes your way is beyond the course of what others have had to face. All you need to remember is that God will never let you down; he'll never let you be pushed past your limit; he'll always be there to help you come through it.

(1 Corinthians 10:13 Msg)

The day I began writing this section of the book, the Lord gave me a new revelation of the storms of life. Like so many others, I attributed the storms of life to traumatic situations like financial difficulty, sickness, death of a loved one, divorce, and painful relationships. Yet today, the Lord showed me another stormy area of my life and that is of my singleness. A moment of transparency forces me to reveal a sincere longing, my deep desire to share my life with someone, a man who has a heart for God and for me. In my journey of singleness, I have had some clear misses and some near misses, men who looked like the one and others I knew were not the one right away. I know that I'm not alone in my desire for a mate and I know I'm not alone in my desire to please the Lord while I wait. The journey gets difficult sometimes and the temptation to do what I want when I want surfaces often. But today, the Spirit reminded me of this scripture. I can and have stood against the temptations that try to take me over the edge, to the limit, into sin. Like me, you are able to stand up under temptation! Take the escape that is divinely available to you. There is one; you may not want to take it because it won't always make you feel good. The escape may cause you to be alone for a season. The escape may feel unusual and uncomfortable. But trust God. Trust in His plan. Trust in the fruit of obedience. Trust in His promises. He wants you to stand just as much as you do and when you stand against the temptations in life, you give Him glory. You can do it!

Personal Reflection

Moses fasted. Elijah fasted 40 days. Paul fasted 14 days. Jesus fasted forty days. If the children of God do not fast, how will we ever fit into the armor of God?

Jentezen Franklin

How Bad Do You Want It

And when He had gone indoors, His disciples asked Him privately, why could not we drive it out? And He replied to them, this kind cannot be driven out by anything but prayer *and fasting.*

Mark 9:28-29 (Amp)

How bad do you want it? How bad do you want deliverance? How bad do you want healing manifested in your body or the body of someone close to you? How bad do you want financial liberty, to be the lender and not the borrower? How bad do you want your marriage restored or your children to walk with the Lord? How bad do you want it? Think about that for a moment. We want God to move in our lives; we want Him to do miraculous things in and through us but oftentimes we aren't prepared or willing to give up anything to receive what we have asked of God. Throughout scripture the power of God was present to heal, win battles, and provide for the needs of His people and more. Yet in this scripture in Mark's gospel, the disciples wanted to know why they couldn't heal a demon possessed boy. They had done it before. Why couldn't they do it this time? Jesus told them that what they were dealing with only comes out by prayer and fasting. Oftentimes, when we need God to really move in our lives, we think prayer alone is enough. We wonder why we haven't seen a change. We wonder why the chains of bondage haven't been broken. A reason could be that whatever you're dealing with will only come out by prayer and fasting. Prayers prayed with the right motives and in the will of God are appropriate. However, when we incorporate fasting we empty ourselves of ourselves so that we can be filled with more of God. Through fasting we see clearer, become: stronger, wise, and better. We gain God's perspective, receive strategies, and anointing to do what He's called us to do or to endure. Fasting requires discipline, denial, and diligence. Fasting and prayer are a powerful duo and according to this scripture, there will be times in your life when you're going to have to turn down your plate and turn your face to God. So I'll ask the question again, how bad do you want it?

Personal Reflection

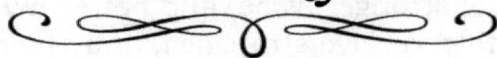

At each state of [spiritual] growth, more self-denial is required, more painful blows to self, more reckless decision to serve the Lord Christ with consequent abandonment of one's own life.

Walter J. Chantry

It's Not About You

"...whoever wants to be my disciple must deny themselves and take up their cross and follow me."

Mark 8:34

The words of this scripture hit me like a truck one day. I was moping, feeling really low. I was ready for my season of suffering (longsuffering in my eyes) to end. I was tired, tired of the same pain, tired of the struggle, tired of the hits. I was just plain old tired. When was God going to come and see about me? When was He going to intervene on my behalf? He'd done it before. Where was He now? I needed Him. Then the Spirit hit me with this scripture! I said, "Ouch Lord!" I was walking around claiming to be a disciple of Christ, going through the motions. I showed up for church, every Sunday. I sang the songs of praise and encouraged people in the Lord along the way. I thought I was a faithful servant yet I had these feelings within. Valid feelings, but feelings just the same. Our feelings don't come from spiritual places, our faith does. Our feelings are about us, our flesh, our wants, our needs. What about me? But Jesus said that if we want to be His disciples we must deny ourselves. We must reject what we want for ourselves and desire what God wants to do for us and through us. What if your pain is accomplishing a spiritual discipline? What if your pain is revealing God's grace and mercy? What if your pain is giving you and others revelations about the kingdom of God that you never had before? Being a disciple of Christ is not about you and it's not about me! Discipleship is about surrender; it's about submission and sacrifice. The kingdom of God is the focus of a true disciple. As soon as we understand these things, we're ready to follow Christ, cross and all.

Personal Reflection

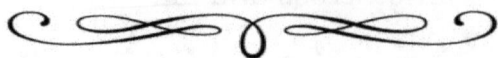

Sometimes, we have to speak peace over ourselves.

Yelva Burley

Encourage Yourself

And David was greatly distressed; for the people spake
of stoning him, because the soul of all the people was
grieved, every man for his sons and for his daughters:
but David encouraged himself in the LORD his God.

1 Samuel 30:6

Standing in and through the storms of life demands that
we grow up in the faith. Those who are immature in the
faith need constant encouragement. They need others to
pray for them or with them. They need others to go to
church with them. They need everyone to be their
friend. But mature saints are people who understand a
thing or two about encouraging themselves in the Lord.
Mature saints, people who really walk with the Lord,
understand that sometimes, a lot of the times, disciples
of Christ are going to have to encourage themselves in
the Lord.

Sometimes no one is going to be around. Sometimes
people just won't be able to understand. Sometimes
people aren't hearing from the Lord on your behalf.
Sometimes the pastor will be out of town and your
prayer partners will be busy fighting their own battles.
Sometimes it's just going to be you and only you.
Beloved, in order to stand and when you've done all, to
just stand, you're going to have to encourage yourself.
The push you need may have to come from within.
Through the power of the Holy Ghost who dwells within
you, you may have to speak life over yourself, over your
family, over your finances, over your health, over your
job. Don't look for people to do it for you. Death and life

is in your tongue (Proverbs 18:21). You have the word of God hidden in your heart. You can declare a thing and see it established (Job 22:28). Learn to and be prepared to encourage yourself!

Personal Reflection

Create in me a pure heart, O God...

Psalm 51:10a

Good Ground

"But the seed falling on good soil refers to someone who hears the word and understands it. This is the one who produces a crop, yielding a hundred, sixty or thirty times what was sown."

Matthew 13:23

Storms have a way of testing things. Storms reveal how good the foundation of a home is. Storms reveal the health and strength of trees. Storms reveal the condition of sewer systems. Storms expose leaks in ceilings. Storms expose things and they expose people. Storms reveal the health and strength of relationships. Storms reveal who's for us and who's against us. And storms expose what kind of ground we are.

The parable of the sower is one of my favorite parables. As a teacher, I love stories and Jesus is an awesome storyteller. Jesus had a way of painting a picture. He was a master of imagery and he knew how to make what he had to say relevant to any audience. Such is the case in this parable. I imagine that his audience knew something about farming. Jesus painted a picture of a farmer going out to sow his seed. As one reads through the parable it's clear that the sower only had one kind of seed. The seed went all over the place but only the seed that fell on good ground yielded a crop. Later in this same chapter Jesus explained the parable. Jesus' explanation is clear; some people just don't have the heart for the word. Therefore, some people just aren't growing in the word. Beloved, you will never survive the storms in life if you aren't growing in the word. Being a way side, a rocky, or a thorny believer will cost you. It will cost you your sanity, your peace, your joy, your relationships, your finances, and an intimate relationship with the One who knows everything you ever did. Are you good ground? Honestly reflect on this question. If your answer is no, repent and return to God. Commit yourself to studying God's word. Submit yourself to God's way- obey His word and eventually, you'll be good ground, ready to stand in and through the storms of life.

Personal Reflection

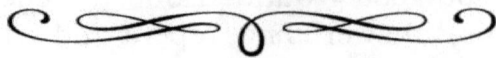

We shall steer safely through every storm, so long as our heart is right, our intention fervent, our courage steadfast, and our trust fixed on God.

St. Francis De Sales

He Will

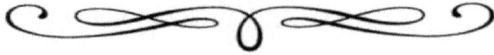

"Because he loves me," says the LORD, "I will rescue him; I will protect him, for he acknowledges my name. He will call on me, and I will answer him; I will be with him in trouble, I will deliver him and honor him. With long life I will satisfy him and show him my salvation."

Psalm 91:14-16

I grew up without an earthly father. I never experienced the comfort of my daddy's arms. My tears were never wiped by the gentle touch of his hands. Advice about boys never reached my itching ears. My wedding day was bitter sweet as I walked down the aisle without him. I missed so much. Well, that's what I thought then. But one day I found my real Father. I found the Man who knew me, who wanted me. I encountered God and since then He's proven that He never leaves and forsakes His children. My Father, God Almighty, is everything I longed for; He's everything I ever needed. The love we share is inseparable; I was made to love Him. He shows up for me. He's present in my victories and He's there with me in my crisis. And guess what, He's there for you too. When the storms of life intensify, when they beat down, reassure yourself that God is there. He's there to bring you out. It's easy to think that God has deserted us when we're going through. People often equate the storms of life to the enemy. The devil may be busy but God is too. Trouble in our lives does not mean God is absent. God is ever-present. He's present in our storms. What I discovered in the stormy seasons of life is what the psalmist wrote: God will rescue us. He's our lifesaver, our lifeguard, our coast guard. He will protect us, from clear and present danger. He will answer us when we cry out for help. He will be with us in trouble. He will deliver us from the chains that bind us. He will honor us because we're humble. He will satisfy us, not withholding any good thing from us because we are determined to walk upright before Him. As much as people love and trust their fathers, the truth is, no earthly father comes close to our God. He will. Let me say it again, He will!

Personal Reflection

What do you do
when you've done all you can
And it seems like it's never enough?
And what do you say
when your friends turn away,
you're all alone?
Tell me, what do you give
When you've given your all,
and seems like
you can't make it through?

Stand and be sure
Be not entangled in that bondage again
You just stand, and be sure.
God has a purpose.
Yes, God has a plan.

Lyrics from "Stand" by Donnie McClurkin

Don't Go Back

It is for freedom that Christ has set us free. Stand firm, then, and do not let yourselves be burdened again by a yoke of slavery.

Galatians 5:1

The enemy doesn't have any new tricks. I remember hearing these words some time ago. Some wise person quoted them and since then, people have being passing this phrase on to describe the predictability of Satan's antics. What are the enemy's tricks? Well, he roams around like a lion – stealing, killing, and destroying. He's a trickster and a deceiver, a major manipulator. He's the author of confusion. He's a counterfeit, masquerading around as a child of light. And because we know who he is and how he operates we shouldn't be surprised when we see him at work. While the devil isn't always the cause of our storms (remember Job), he is always present. The devil prowls around waiting for us to have one of our moments. You know those moments, like when you're in the midst of the storm and you get tired of the fight and you're weary – mentally, physically, and spiritually. You know what I'm talking about. You know those moments when you want to hurt somebody – for real! Storms will make you weak. Storms will make you bitter. Storms will make you crazy, if you let them. The enemy of your soul is waiting for the moment or moments when you are most vulnerable. He's waiting because it's in that place where he can get a foothold, where he can gain access to your mind thereby controlling your behavior. Paul wrote to the believers in Galatia to encourage them during their moments. He encouraged them to stand firm in their faith. It was their faith in Christ that set them free in the first place. Faith in Christ is liberty. Faith in Christ sets captives free. Don't go back to weak and miserable ways. Fear isn't an option. Sin isn't an option. Doubt isn't an option. Christ set you free, once and for all; don't go back. He died that we might have life and live life in all its fullness. Don't go back. Move forward today. Move forward in faith and in Him.

Personal Reflection

God loves to pour out His Spirit with power on those who will dare to align radically their purposes with His.

Steve Childers

Do It God's Way

Commit your way to the LORD; trust in him and he will do this...

Psalm 37:5

There is peace in the will of God. There is purpose in the will of God. There is power in the will of God. Yet, many disciples of Christ can attest to the fact that there's often a great struggle resolving to be in the will of God, to actually live in the will of God. Jesus shows us this in the Garden of Gethsemane. Jesus' prayer in the garden is so raw and so real. Here we have Jesus, the son of God, Emmanuel, the one who turned water into wine, the one who fed 5,000 with two fish and five loaves of bread. Jesus, our Lord, struggled with His Father's will. I love Him for that! I love the fact that Jesus, fully God and fully human, shows us that committing our way to the Lord is difficult. Jesus shows us that doing thing's God's way is not easy, in fact, it may cost you everything. Doing things God's way requires the child of God to intentionally go against what he or she wants for the plan of God. Doing things God's way may require us to go places we don't want to go or to leave places we don't want to leave. Doing things God's way may require us to be still and know that He is God or it may require that we go to a place that He will show us. Doing things God's way requires faith in God, faith in His purpose, faith in His methods, and faith in His timing. So you have some plans? Then commit your way to the Lord. Don't get frustrated if He thwarts you plan, if He says to do it another way or says not to do it at all. Stay on His course, on the road that He laid out for you. Trust Him along the way and you will reach your intended destination. Resolve in your

mind and in your spirit that God's way is the only way
for you.

Personal Reflection

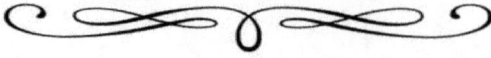

For to me, to live is Christ and to die is gain.

Philippians 1:21

Get Ready to Die

I have been crucified with Christ and I no longer live, but Christ lives in me. The life I now live in the body, I live by faith in the Son of God, who loved me and gave himself for me.

Galatians 2:20

One night I was driving home from church and I heard a song on the radio. The introduction took my breath away. I heard these words, "If I lost everything but still had Jesus, I'd have enough to start all over again." I cried sitting in my car that night. In my estimation, I had lost a lot. This song was a balm for me. It was my release from the disappointment of my circumstances, the disappointment and humiliation of what I thought made me who I am. These lyrics reignited a fire in me, a fire to continue fighting the good fight of faith. These few words reminded me that my life in Christ is more than my possessions. My life in Christ is more than a car, a home, my financial status, or the spouse I desired. My life in Christ is more than anything I can see or touch. My life in Christ is about freedom from condemnation. My life in Christ is about reconciliation with my heavenly Father, the one who wants to spend forever with me. My life in Christ is about service, laying down my life for my brother or sister. My life in Christ is about love, unconditional love. My life in Christ is about forgiveness (even my enemies). My freedom and your freedom in Christ is glorious but I must warn you; it's costly. Its value is priceless yet expensive. The freedom we have in Christ requires that we die in order to live. That sounds like a contradiction but it's true. Christians can't be materialistic. Real Christians understand that living begins once we die to our flesh, die to the life we lived before Christ. Real living begins once we die to the things, attitudes, and behaviors of the world. Real living begins when we take up our cross and follow Him. Once we accept this reality, our "things" and the people we thought we needed won't matter so much anymore. We can live with or without them. Once we resolve within our hearts that, to live is Christ and to die is gain, we are truly free. Then, we can stand – whether we have or whether we lack. Live doesn't really begin until we spiritually die.

Personal Reflection

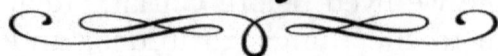

Hide me from circumstances
Hide me when I want to take one more
chance
Hide me when my strength is weak
Hide me when my eyes want to take one
more glance...Hide me...Even if the enemy
you hide, is me

Hide Me
Lyrics by Bruce Parham

Hide Me

He will cover you with his feathers, and under his wings
you will find refuge; his faithfulness will be your shield
and rampart.

Psalm 91:4

Exhausted from the battle? Has your war lasted longer
than you expected? Are you fatigued, hungry for change
or desperately needing time and space to regain your
strength? Are you tired of meeting the needs of others
while your needs go unsatisfied. Are you tired of trying
to meet the expectations of others? I've been where you
are? I know what it's like to want to disappear, to go
missing. I know what it's like to want to escape life, to
want to take a vacation and never come back. I
understand. But most importantly, God understands.
God knows exactly where you are. He knows what
you're thinking. He knows what you're not saying. He
knows the secrets of your heart. He hears your faintest
cries. And He cares. God left His word to comfort
weather-beaten souls. It's in the word of God that we
see the Lord's care and compassion for the weary. He
reminds us that we don't have to run to alcohol, to
drugs, to another bed, to food or any other placebo to
help us cope with life. He is our hiding place. He allows
us to come to Him when we need to get away, when we
need to hide from the storms and stormy people in our
lives. He reminds us that we can come to and
experience the safety of His presence, to discover that
He is our refuge and strength. He'll shield us from the
effects of the storm. Won't you let Him? Won't you let
Him hide you?

Personal Reflection

Because Jesus is "THE DOOR," He is able to open doors for you that no man can shut and He's able to create doors where no door exists. (John 10:7)
You're getting up in there!

Yelva Burley

Relentless

"Ask and it will be given to you; seek and you will find; knock and the door will be opened to you. For everyone who asks receives; the one who seeks finds; and to the one who knocks, the door will be opened.

Matthew 7:7-8

So, you know the promises of God. You stand on them. So, you're in the will of God. You strive to live righteously before Him. Your motives are pure. You confessed your sins and the Lord created in you a clean heart and renewed the right spirit within you. So what's the problem? When is your change 'gon come? I can't give you a timeline on your deliverance but I can tell you with confidence that a change will come. We don't get to schedule our date of deliverance. However, we do have an assurance that something is going to happen; we just have to remain relentless. This is the word the Spirit gave me as I was meditating on Matthew 7:7-8. I love the word of God but I especially love the words of my Savior. In these passages, Jesus is continuing what some call His Sermon on the Mount. It is here where we receive comfort and instruction for our weary souls. These passages of scripture are fuel to keep on keeping on. It is the bread that hungry souls need to feast on. These passages let us know that we haven't done enough and that we haven't done it all. Another translation of this scripture says to "keep on asking...keep on seeking...and keep on knocking." That's being relentless. To keep on "doing" while we're waiting on God is not easy. To keep on asking, seeking, and knocking may seem foolish to others but it must never seem foolish to you. Jesus promised that those

145

who ask will receive. Those who seek will find and those who knock will have a door opened for them.

Relentlessness acknowledges the facts but it allows faith to prevail. Relentlessness gives fresh strength to weary bones. Relentlessness is a testimony, all by itself. Relentlessness believes, hopes, and dreams.

Relentlessness doesn't stop; it doesn't quit.

Relentlessness won't let go until the Lord blesses. So be relentless; it pays off!

Personal Reflection

There is still life left in you.

Yelva Burley

Stop the Pity Party

We are hard pressed on every side, but not crushed;
perplexed, but not in despair; persecuted, but not
abandoned; struck down, but not destroyed. We always
carry around in our body the death of Jesus, so that the
life of Jesus may also be revealed in our body.

2 Corinthians 4:8-10

I was at the gym when I first heard about the senseless
bombings at the Boston Marathon. What started as a
normal Monday turned out to be anything but normal.
At the writing of this devotion, the authorities continue
to question the surviving suspect, piece together pieces
of their plan of terror, and investigate the suspects' ties
to other terrorist groups. The events of that fateful
Monday still have people talking. What amazed me
about the events of that day and the days after were the
stories of those who survived the bombing. Many of the
victims lost limbs that day and are now facing a new
normal. Their lives changed that day, some believe for
the worse. Yet, several of the survivors who were
interviewed spoke with such hope and gratitude to be
alive. There language was not the language of the
defeated. The survivors that I saw spoke with a sense of
peace, an assurance that life is not over for them. We
call them victims but they really are victors. These
people chose to do something that every person must
chose to do when faced with a crisis. They chose to live
beyond the day. These men and women chose to live
beyond the moment that changed their lives forever.
These men and women chose to live beyond the chaos
and fear. They chose to live. And that's what we must do
when we face trials of many kinds. The pity parties need
to be shut down. Those semi-deflated balloons need to

149

be popped and trashed. It's time to move on. It's time to believe again, dream again, pursue again, and live again. This change of mind doesn't occur overnight. This change of mind occurs when the one having the pity party decides that living a miserable life is not living. A change will occur when the decision is made to look up and not down anymore. A change will surface once we've moved beyond pathetic to praise.

The Apostle Paul is the epitome of a survivor. He survived persecution, threats, beatings, imprisonments, and more, yet he had enough Christ in him to encourage the believers in Corinth with these words, "We are hard pressed on every side, but not crushed; perplexed, but not in despair; persecuted, but not abandoned; struck down, but not destroyed." Reality is reality. Don't deny that life has you in a rough place. But don't accept that today's reality has to stop tomorrow's reasons for living.

Personal Reflection

Do not be anxious about anything, but in every situation, by prayer and petition, with thanksgiving, present your requests to God. And the peace of God, which transcends all understanding, will guard your hearts and your minds in Christ Jesus.

Philippians 4:6-7

Bipolar

For God did not give us a spirit of timidity (of cowardice, of craven and cringing and fawning fear), but [He has given us a spirit] of power and of love and of calm *and* well-balanced mind *and* discipline *and* self-control.
2 Timothy 1:7(Amp)

I can't speak from anyone else's life experiences but I have to admit that while I endured some of the storms in my life, I sometimes felt quite bipolar. One moment I was up and the next I was down. There were some mornings I woke up and believed that better was coming and then there were mornings when I woke up with dread and fear about what the day would bring. Some days were just laborious. The labor of the day wasn't actual work from employment. For me, during these seasons, work was the face I made up for people. It was the face that I knew people could handle. You do know that some people can't handle your mood swings. So, I put on a happy face and went about life day after day. There were many days that I struggled to keep up the act. There were days when I couldn't fake it. These days I call my bipolar days. There's no disrespect to those who suffer with this mental disease. I just liken my mental and spiritual state during the storms of my life as up one moment and drastically down the next. The word of God reminds us that our mood swings are spiritual. Our enemy loves to mess with our minds and it's for this reason we're armed with the spirit of a well-balanced mind. In addition to the spirit of power, love, discipline, and self-control, the Father graciously bestows upon His children the spirit of a calm, well-balanced mind. God is so in tune with us. He sees our struggle. He knows our heart. He knows our heart's cry. And that's why He provides us with the mind that keeps everything else going. With our calm, well-balanced mind, we can discern truth. With our calm, well-balanced mind, the Holy Spirit reminds us that our trouble isn't permanent. A calm, well-balanced mind is critical in our journey of standing through the storms in our lives. Receive yours today, in Jesus name.

Personal Reflection

"Ah, Sovereign LORD, you have made the heavens and the earth by your great power and outstretched arm. Nothing is too hard for you."

Jeremiah 32:17

Look Up

I lift up my eyes to the mountains— where does my help
come from? My help comes from the LORD,   the Maker
of heaven and earth. He will not let your foot slip—he
who watches over you will not slumber; indeed, he who
watches over Israel will neither slumber nor sleep.

Psalm 121:1-4

This is a psalm about protection, about the Lord's
keeping power when we're in need. These words comfort
those in need of the Lord's touch and serve as a
reminder of several things. The first thing this psalm
reminds us of is where our help comes from. Our help
does not come from earthly places or people. Our help
comes from above. Therefore, in order to secure the help
we need, we must look up. The Lord, who made heaven
and earth is up. Our bowed down, sorrowful heads
must look up to see and hear from God. The second
thing this psalm reminds us of is that the Lord won't let
us fail. He won't let our feet slip. Our definition of failure
and God's definition of failure is different. In Christ, we
are victorious, more than conquerors. In Christ, we can
do all things. Therefore, our mishaps
and mistakes aren't failures. They serve as
opportunities for us to remember that we need God.
Therefore, we look up. The third thing that this psalm
reminds us of is that God knows. He knows all about
our troubles.

We know where our help comes from. We are not
failures; He will not let our foot slip. God is on the case.
While we're tossing and turning, trying to rest, the Lord,

never rests; He doesn't need sleep. He's ready to take control of our situations. He doesn't need to get refreshed or renewed. He doesn't need eight hours of sleep to recover. Be comforted today that help is available. You just have to look up to see Him.

Personal Reflection

The LORD is close to the brokenhearted
and saves those who are crushed in spirit.
The righteous person may have many
troubles, but the LORD delivers him from
them all...

Psalm 34:18-19

Go to Jesus

"Come to me, all you who are weary and burdened, and I will give you rest. Take my yoke upon you and learn from me, for I am gentle and humble in heart, and you will find rest for your souls. For my yoke is easy and my burden is light."

Matthew 11:28-30

We are living in a day in age where the number of life coaches and "fixers" is rising. From television shows where people specialize in fixing other people's messes to cable programs that focus on people and families that have relational issues that need to be fixed. Although the television dramas aren't real life stories, they often depict situations that are close to home: infidelity, abuse, secrets, conspiracies, and the like. People are seeking, seeking help, answers, hope, resolution, and reconciliation. Unfortunately, the "fixers" in the world provide temporary fixes. Their sphere of influence is limited. Their knowledge of the deep and spiritual issues that are at the root of people's drama can't be fixed during a 60 minute program. Deep and spiritual issues can only be fixed by the One who created Heaven and earth. All we have to do is just come to Him. Oh the rest we would enjoy and the peace that would flood our hearts if we'd remember to first come to the Lord. We wouldn't waste time with people who are wise in their own eyes. We wouldn't lose sleep. The hairs on our head would remain in tack. We wouldn't be snappy and irritable, if we'd only do what Jesus told us to do. When we cast all our cares on Him we find rest for our souls. He can handle whatever we face. He wants to carry our heavy loads. We just have to come to Him and let our stuff go.

Personal Reflection

You Lord, You alone are my heart's song. I will sing of your love forever and ever and ever.

Yelva Burley

You Gave Me A New Song

I waited patiently for the LORD to help me, and he
turned to me and heard my cry. He lifted me out of the
pit of despair, out of the mud and the mire. He set my
feet on solid ground and steadied me as I walked along.
He has given me a new song to sing, a hymn of praise to
our God. Many will see what he has done and be
amazed. They will put their trust in the LORD.

Psalm 40:1-3

God doesn't withhold hard times from His children. In
fact, disciples of Christ often face more intense struggles
because they belong to God. I remember a time when I
struggled with where I was in my journey of faith.
During this season, I struggled hard and long. I lost a
lot of things. I lost the joy of the Lord. I moved about the
days routinely, without the peace of God. And I lost my
song. I am a worshipper and one way that I often
worship God is through song. I don't have a voice like
an angel but when I sing a song of Zion, I know that I
touch the heart of God. I love to exhort the Lord with
my mouth. But during this difficult time, no song came
to my heart nor from my lips. I couldn't fake it. My
heart didn't beat with His and I couldn't sing about His
goodness. It can happen. It can happen to those
who've walked with God a long time. It can happen to
those new in Christ and to those who've been on the
battle field for a long time. It's easy to lose your song.
Psalm 40 shows us how we lose our song. The first way
is to grow impatient with God. The second way is to
think that God doesn't care, to think that He is ignorant
of our cries, of our sorrow. A third way is to toy with
the idea that God will allow us to fail, to stumble. The

Psalmist turned his distress into a song of praise, a new song. You can too. You don't have to lose your song in the storm. In fact, I leave you with the following song by Douglas Miller. You can and will weather the storms of life, strong, like a tree, only if your soul is anchored in the Lord.

Personal Reflection

My Soul Has Been Anchored
Douglas Miller

Though the storms keep on raging in my life;
And sometimes it's hard to tell the night from day;
Still that hope that lies within is reassured
As I keep my eyes upon the distant shore;
I know He'll lead me safely to that blessed place He has
prepared.

But if the storms don't cease,
And if the winds keep on blowing in my life,
My soul has been anchored in the Lord.

Oh, I realize that sometimes in this life we're gonna be
tossed,
by the waves and the currents that seem so fierce, but
in the word of God I've got an anchor
and it keeps me steadfast and unmovable despite the
tide,

But if the storms don't cease,
and if the winds keep on blowing in my life,
my soul has been anchored in the Lord.

My souls been, my souls been anchored,
my souls been anchored, my, my, my, my, my soul;

Billiards may roll;
Breakers may dash;
I shall not sway because He holds me back;
So dark the days, that lies in the sky;
But I know it's all right 'cause Jesus is mine;
Say my soul, my soul;

My soul has been anchored in the, in the Lord.

Personal Reflection

A Final Word to Stand on...

It's Coming

Then they cried out to the LORD in their trouble,
and he delivered them from their distress.
He led them by a straight way
to a city where they could settle.

Psalm 107:6-7

This book was sent off to my editing team because I thought it was finished. I didn't know that God had other plans with this project. Have you ever had a moment when you thought you'd completed everything God asked you to do then you hear Him say, "I need more?" Well, that's why there's a "final word" in this book. This word came to me during a prayer moment with my church family. This scripture was the word for the day and I clearly heard God say, "This is you, this is your testimony." Like A Tree is my testimony. It is the word of God and my testimony for the building up of others. I cried to the Lord. Like A Tree is my lament. It's my celebration, my moments of self encouragement, my victories, my struggles - not for me but for others. My season of struggle ended. I was delivered; I am still being delivered. The Lord brought me to a beautiful place in my life, a place of liberty and hope. I'm settled in a new land today, a land where I'm free to be me. I love my new home. I'm content - whether with plenty or in lack. I'm loved - confident that nothing can separate me from the love of God. This is your story too isn't it? By the grace of God you'll be able to stand in your storms, encouraged, empowered, and equipped to outlast your storm and bear fruit in your storm. Your season of struggle will come to an end. You'll see how God heard your cries. You'll see how he has delivered you. You'll experience His guidance and His settling. Trust me; it's coming!

Personal Reflection

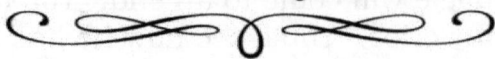

Contact the Author

Beloved,

Please let me know how this book has been a blessing in your life. We overcome by the blood of the Lamb and by the word of our testimony (Revelation 12:11). I want to hear your story. I want to rejoice with you; I want to celebrate with you. We are all, Like A Tree, standing by the rivers of water, producing fruit, in season.

Peace and Blessings,

Yelva

You can reach me via postal mail, Twitter, Facebook, or by email.

Speak Life Publishing, LLC
P.O. Box 1144
Baltimore, MD 21203

Twitter: @yelvab

Facebook: www.facebook.com/ysburley

Email: ysburley@hotmail.com

174